Exploring Citizenship

Fair Play

Sue Barraclough

Heinemann
LIBRARY

www.heinemannlibrary.co.uk
Visit our website to find out more information about Heinemann Library books.

To order:
☎ Phone +44 (0) 1865 888066
🖷 Fax +44 (0) 1865 314091
💻 Visit www.heinemannlibrary.co.uk

©Heinemann Library is an imprint of Capstone Global Library Limited, a company incorporated in England and Wales having its registered office at 7 Pilgrim Street, London, EC4V 6LB - Registered company number: 6695582

"Heinemann" is a registered trademark of Pearson Education Limited, under licence to Capstone Global Library Limited

Text © Capstone Global Library Limited 2010
First published in hardback in 2010

Edited by Charlotte Guillain and Catherine Veitch
Designed by Ryan Frieson and Betsy Wernert
Picture research by Elizabeth Alexander and Rebecca Sodergren
Production by Duncan Gilbert
Originated by Heinemann Library
Printed in China by South China Printing Company Ltd

ISBN 978 0 431 02539 1
14 13 12 11 10
10 9 8 7 6 5 4 3 2 1

British Library Cataloguing in Publication Data
Barraclough, Sue
Fair play. – (Exploring citizenship)
302.1'4
A full catalogue record for this book is available from the British Library.

Acknowledgements

We would like to thank the following for permission to reproduce photographs: Alamy **pp. 7** (© Ben Molyneux People), **13** (© Photostockfile), **18** (© Radius Images); © Corbis **9**; Corbis **pp 4** (© SW Productions/Brand X), **5** (© Jim Craigmyle), **6** (© Randy Faris), **8** (© Image Source), **12** (© Lawrence Manning), **20** (© Everett Kennedy Brown/EPA), **22** (© Diego Azubel/epa), **26** (© William Manning); Getty Images **pp. 10** (Julian Finney), **11** (Corey Davis), **15** (Nikolaevich/Taxi), **17** (Jim Doberman/Taxi), **19** (Sandra Behne/Bongarts), **23** (Jim McIsaac), **24** (Dean Treml/Stringer/AFP), **27** (JJ/Taxi), **29** (Symphonie/Iconica); PA Photos **p. 14** (Christof Stache/AP); Photolibrary **p. 16** (Corbis).

Cover photograph of football teams exchanging handshakes reproduced with permission of Corbis (© Fancy/Veer).

We would like to thank Yael Biederman for her help in the preparation of this book.

Every effort has been made to contact copyright holders of material reproduced in this book. Any omissions will be rectified in subsequent printings if notice is given to the publishers.

All the Internet addresses (URLs) given in this book were valid at the time of going to press. However, due to the dynamic nature of the Internet, some addresses may have changed, or sites may have changed or ceased to exist since publication. While the author and publisher regret any inconvenience this may cause readers, no responsibility for any such changes can be accepted by either the author or the publisher.

Contents

Some words are shown in bold, **like this**. You can find out what they mean by looking in the glossary.

What is citizenship?

Citizenship is about being a member of a group. A group can be a family, a class, a team, or a country. A citizen has certain **rights** and **responsibilities**.

Every member of a group should be treated fairly.

Having rights means that other people should treat you in a certain way. Having responsibilities means you should act or behave in a certain way towards others.

A good citizen makes sure that no one feels left out.

What is fair play?

Fair play is a way of acting or behaving when you are playing games or sports. Fair play is understanding that how you act is important and affects others.

Fair play is being friendly and polite to other players.

Whatever the game, you should always expect others to play fairly.

You have a **responsibility** to act in a **fair** way. You also have a **right** to be treated in a fair way by others.

Respecting others

Listening to the referee is part of playing fairly.

Fair play is also about **respecting** others, such as players, coaches, referees, and spectators. Everyone has the **right** to take part and to be treated with respect.

Fair play is taking time to listen and understand what you are being told. Coaches and teachers have knowledge and experience to share. All the players in a team should be able to tell each other what they think.

Respect is treating people in a fair and friendly way.

Playing by the rules

Fair play is about understanding that **rules** are useful. Rules about how to play games and what to wear have been **agreed** by everyone. Rules make games and sports safer.

Each sport has its own set of rules.

It is important that everyone agrees to play in a certain way. Everyone should agree to play by the same rules. Everyone should agree that the rules are **fair**.

Good rules are fair to everyone.

Breaking the rules

Sometimes you want to win so badly that you forget to play **fairly**. Sometimes you forget the **rules** and do something that is not allowed.

Referees watch to make sure play is fair.

Fair play is about owning up to mistakes or saying sorry if you have done something wrong. You should always:
- say sorry when you need to
- help another player if they are hurt
- try not to shout or get angry.

The referee decides when rules are broken.

What is cheating?

Cheating is breaking the **rules**. It is choosing to play unfairly to win.

Would you feel happy if you had cheated to win?

14

It is your **responsibility** as part of the team to stick to the rules of the game.

If you cheat or break the rules, other people may not see you or find out. But even if they do not find out, you will know. Even if you win, this can stop you feeling happy.

Controlling your feelings

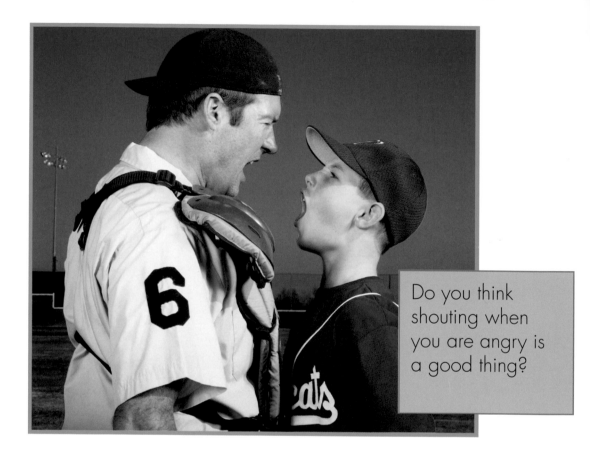

Do you think shouting when you are angry is a good thing?

Sometimes you may feel upset or angry about something that has happened in a game. You may get knocked, hit, or pushed by other players. Try not to take it personally. Do your best to carry on and play well.

If you play **fairly** you do not shout, **swear**, or make fun of other players. If you play fairly you do not hit back or argue with other players. You can try to use all your energy to play as well as you can.

How would you feel if someone shouted at you?

Talking it through

If you see someone cheat or play unfairly, talk to the coach or the referee about it during or after the match. Try not to shout or argue with other players or adults.

How do you think the referee feels when he is shouted at?

Do you think this is a better way to talk to a referee?

Remember that you can take part to change things. You should talk about things you do not like. It is important that you follow **rules** and behave well because you think it is right and you agree with the rules.

Helping others

Treat other players as you would like to be treated yourself. If someone trips and falls over, they will feel better if you help them up.

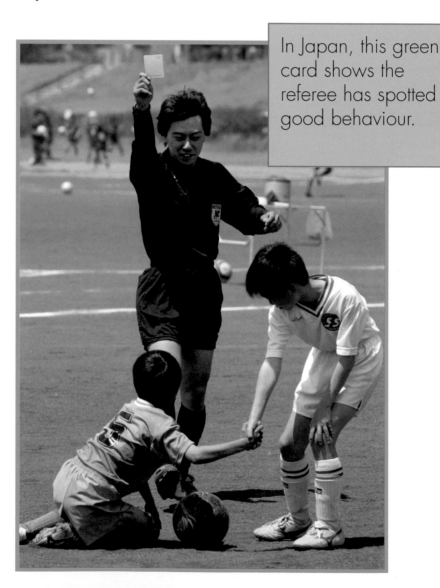

In Japan, this green card shows the referee has spotted good behaviour.

Fair play is about being a good team player. Good team players try to win as part of the team rather than just for themselves.

A good team player:

- **encourages** teammates
- cheers good play
- plays **fairly** and follows the **rules**
- does their best for the team
- works with and helps others
- **communicates** well
- acts in a cheerful, friendly way.

Good role models

Good role models are **modest** when they win.

Sporting **skill** alone does not make someone a good player and **role model**. A good role model is one who plays well and **fairly**. A good role model is fair and friendly to other players.

Sometimes famous sports stars behave badly. Do not copy this poor behaviour even if someone is your sporting hero. Players who fight or argue during a game or match are bad role models.

Win or lose, a good role model is friendly and polite.

Winning and losing

Everyone likes to win. We all feel good when we win a game or a race. Sharing success with teammates is an especially good feeling.

How do you feel when you win?

If you lose you might feel unhappy. Fair play is about behaving well even if you lose, and clapping the winners. The other player or team won because they played better, so you can try to play better next time.

Tips for how to be a good loser:

- try to control your feelings
- say "well done" to the winning player or team
- say "thank you" to judges, referees, and other officials.

Is fair play important?

Fair play makes you feel good about yourself. Fair play will make others **respect** and trust you. If you play **fairly** you will be a good **role model**.

Fair play is telling other team members that they have done well.

Being part of a team can help you make good friendships with others.

Fair play is important because it means sports and games can be fun for everyone. Having fun and making friends is more important than winning.

Play fair and have fun

Fair play is having fun and learning new **skills**. Fair play makes you feel good and makes sport and games safer and **fairer** for everyone.

Fair play checklist

- ☑ follow **agreed rules**
- ☑ take turns and share
- ☑ **respect** others
- ☑ help others
- ☑ try to control your feelings
- ☑ be **modest** when you win
- ☑ be **generous** when you lose.

It makes you feel proud to have played your best, and played fairly. It feels good to be part of a team.

It is fun to win when you have worked together as a team.

Glossary

agreed when two or more people have decided something is good or right

communicate speak and listen

encourage act or behave in a way that helps someone do something

fair way of behaving that treats everyone equally and that everyone is happy with

generous kind and giving to others

modest not boasting or showing off

respect way of treating someone or something with kindness, politeness, and care

responsibility something that it is your job to do as a good and useful member of a group

right how you should be treated by others, in a way that is thought to be good or fair by most people

role model someone you admire. A role model is a person whose behaviour you try to copy.

rule something that says how things should be done, and tells you what you are allowed or not allowed to do

skill able to do something well

swear say rude words

Find out more

Books

Citizenship: Being Responsible, Cassie Mayer (Heinemann Library, 2007)

Citizenship: Following Rules, Cassie Mayer (Heinemann Library, 2008)

Websites

www.timeforcitizenship.org/citizenship.php
You can see what other children think about citizenship on this web page.

www.gogivers.org
This animated site shows children what it means to be part of a caring society.

Index